Nana's Herb Garden

by Frances Ferrara Alvear
Illustrated by Susan Spellman

PEARSON

Glenview, Illinois • Boston, Massachusetts • Chandler, Arizona
Upper Saddle River, New Jersey

spaghetti
and meatballs

Nana lived in Italy before she moved to New York. She moved to New York to live near her son and his wife. She wanted to live near her granddaughters, Donna and Teresa.

Donna and Teresa loved Nana. They loved to help Nana cook. They loved to help her cook spaghetti and meatballs!

One day Nana looked sad. "Why are you unhappy?" asked the girls.

"Well," said Nana, "I love being here with you. I love cooking spaghetti and meatballs with you. I just miss my herb garden in Italy. It is so beautiful in my herb garden at this time of year."

"What is an herb garden?" the girls asked.

"Herbs are plants," said Nana. "I grow them in my herb garden. The herbs look beautiful and they smell good. People use herbs to add flavor to food. In Italy, I snipped herbs from my garden to use when I cooked."

---

flavor: taste   **snipped:** cut off

herbs

Nana's herb garden in Italy

Parsley is an herb.

Basil is an herb.

Parsley, basil, rosemary, and oregano are all herbs. Nana grew parsley, basil, rosemary, and oregano in her herb garden. She added oregano and basil to spaghetti sauce. She added rosemary to chicken. She added parsley to many foods.

Rosemary is an herb.

Oregano is an herb.

Donna and Teresa recognized the names of some of these herbs. "We know where we can get some herbs for you!" they shouted. "Mom buys them at the supermarket."

"Thank you," said Nana. "But those herbs are dried. They are not fresh herbs. I like to put fresh herbs in the food I cook. That is why I miss my garden!"

---

supermarket: big grocery store

window

seedlings

The girls decided to plant an herb garden for Nana. They went with their parents to buy a window box, a bag of soil, and herb seedlings.

Dad put the window box outside the kitchen window. Mom filled the box with soil. They helped the girls plant the seedlings. Then the girls watered the window box.

---

window box: a box for plants that hangs in a window

seedlings: tiny new plants (baby plants)

herbs

Nana was surprised and happy! Before long, the new herbs came up. They grew tall and strong. Whenever Nana cooked, she snipped fresh herbs. She taught the girls how to use the herbs when she cooked.

Nana's window box garden made the whole family happy!

Would you like to make a surprise for someone special?

The Eagle,
A Symbol of
Freedom

by Tiffany Gibson

PEARSON

Glenview, Illinois • Boston, Massachusetts
Chandler Arizona • Upper Saddle River, New Jersey

heart

stop sign

Symbols

You can find symbols all around you. Symbols are shapes, colors, and pictures that mean something.

When we see a symbol, we think of what it means. We know a red sign means stop. A heart is another symbol. We think of love when we see it.

bald eagle

American flag

Countries have symbols too. A flag is a symbol. The United States has a flag. It also has other symbols.

The bald eagle is an American symbol. The bald eagle stands for, or means, freedom. Freedom means you can make your own decisions.

---

freedom: the right to do want you want

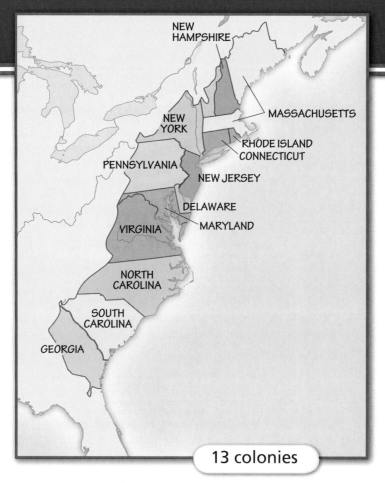

13 colonies

Early America

How did the United States pick the bald eagle? In 1782, there were 13 colonies in America. There were colonies before there were states.

England made the *laws* in the colonies. Laws are rules. The people in the colonies did not like these laws. They wanted freedom to make their own rules.

---

colonies: areas of land that later became the United States

Leaders of the 13 colonies

Leaders from each colony met. They decided to make a new country. The new country was the United States of America.

They needed a symbol to show what the new country believed in. The United States believed in freedom. The leaders wanted to show that this new country was free from England.

The leaders wanted an animal for the symbol. They wanted one with courage. They picked one that lived in the United States. They picked the bald eagle.

The Great Seal

The leaders used the eagle in the Great Seal. The seal is like a stamp. Leaders used the stamp on papers and letters.

Leaders still use this stamp today.

---

courage: the ability to be brave

Franklin wanted a turkey
for America's symbol.

National Turkey?

One of the leaders in the first 13 colonies was Benjamin Franklin. He wanted a different national symbol.

He thought the eagle was lazy. He also thought the eagle was not honest. Franklin wanted a turkey for the national symbol.

Today, the bald eagle is still a symbol of freedom. You can find the eagle on a one-dollar bill. You can find it on coins. The eagle is on some stamps. It is also used on the President's seal.

Look around today. Where can you find America's symbol for freedom?